THE **Salem** WITCH TRIALS

SPOT THE MYTHS

T0008949

by Megan Cooley Peterson

CAPSTONE PRESS
a capstone imprint

Published by Capstone Press, an imprint of Capstone
1710 Roe Crest Drive, North Mankato, Minnesota 56003
capstonepub.com

Library of Congress Cataloging-in-Publication Data is available
on the Library of Congress website.
ISBN: 9781669062561 (hardcover)
ISBN: 9781669062745 (paperback)
ISBN: 9781669062592 (ebook PDF)

Summary: Starting in 1692, many American colonists accused others
of being witches in Salem, Massachusetts. It resulted in the deaths of
several innocent people. Myths about the Salem witch trials have stuck
around for hundreds of years. Now it's up to you to separate the truths
from the myths. Will you be able to guess them? Or will you be fooled?

Editorial Credits
Editor: Carrie Sheely; Designer: Bobbie Nuytten; Media Researcher:
Rebekah Hubstenberger; Production Specialist: Whitney Schaefer

Image Credits
Alamy: Classic Image, 21, North Wind Picture Archives, 11; Getty
Images: Jim Davis/The Boston Globe, 29, mikroman6, 13, MPI,
Cover, 15, Nastasic, 19, Photos.com, 25; Library of Congress: Prints
and Photographs Division, 6; Shutterstock: Apostrophe, design
element (texture), Arthur Balitskii, design element (witch icons),
cindylindowphotography, 4, 24, Everett Collection, 7, 9, 17, 27, Manfred
Ruckszio, 22, OlgaChernyak, design element (wolf)

TABLE OF CONTENTS

What Really Happened in Salem? 4

The Accused 6

How Fear Shaped the Trials 10

The Court 14

Evidence and Punishments 18

How Food Played a Role 22

After the Trials 26

Glossary 30
Read More 31
Internet Sites 31
Index 32
About the Author 32

Words in **bold** are in the glossary.

What Really Happened in Salem?

It's January 1692. It seems like an ordinary day in Salem, a town in the British Massachusetts Bay **Colony** in North America. The home of minister Samuel Parris takes a dark turn. His daughter, Betty, and niece, Abigail Williams, act strangely. They cry out. Their bodies twist. They say unseen hands pinch and hit them. A doctor decides it must be witchcraft. Soon, the girls **accuse** three women of using witchcraft to hurt them.

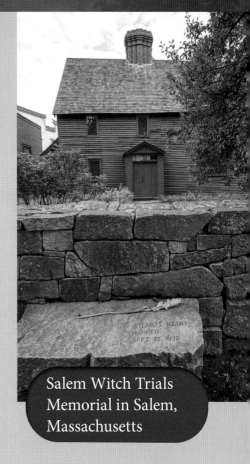

Salem Witch Trials Memorial in Salem, Massachusetts

Complaints of witchcraft flew fast and furious in Salem more than 300 years ago. Today, we know the **trials** were unfair. But how much do you know about what happened? Journey through Salem in 1692. Meet the people who shaped the events. Three statements will be presented together. But only two are true. Try to decide what's truth and what's a myth. How well will you play the game?

HOW CAN I TELL WHAT'S TRUTH AND WHAT'S A MYTH?

START HERE. ⇨ Does the statement include words like "all" or "none"?

YES ⇨ It might be a myth. Words such as "all" or "none" often simplify complicated topics. These statements might not be true.

NO ⇨ Does the statement include specific information, such as names or dates?

YES ⇨ It might be true. Details are important when dealing with facts. The more details a statement provides, the more likely it is to be true.

NO ⇨ It might be a myth. Vague facts without detail might be made up. It's good to question statements that don't include specific details.

The Accused

1. ONLY WOMEN WERE ACCUSED OF WITCHCRAFT IN SALEM.

In the British colonies, women had less power than men. A married woman's property belonged to her husband. Women couldn't vote or serve on juries. Men made the colony's rules.

In Salem, accusations of witchcraft led to tense trials in 1692.

2. CHILDREN AS YOUNG AS 4 WERE LOCKED UP FOR WITCHCRAFT.

Dorothy Good was 4 years old when she was accused of witchcraft. Her mother, Sarah Good, was one of the first arrested. Dorothy **confessed** so she could be with her mother in jail.

3. DURING THE TRIALS, TWO DOGS WERE ACCUSED OF BEING WITCHES.

Accusers in Salem and the nearby town Andover said bewitched dogs hurt them. The dogs were killed. Minister Cotton Mather later said they were ordinary dogs. He said a bewitched animal can't be killed.

Cotton Mather

THE MYTH

ONLY WOMEN WERE ACCUSED OF WITCHCRAFT.

With less power, women were more likely to be accused. But men also faced charges. At least eight men were accused, and six were put to death. Sarah Good and Sarah Osborn were two of the first people to be accused. Sarah Good's family was homeless. She begged for food and shelter. Sarah Osborn was sick. She hadn't been to church in more than a year. This made people distrust her. A woman **enslaved** by Samuel Parris named Tituba was also accused. The practice of enslaving non-white people and forcing them to do work was common in the colonies.

FACT

Bridget Bishop was the first to be killed during the trials. She had been accused of witchcraft and stealing years earlier.

Other suspects were also named. John and Elizabeth Proctor owned a farm and a tavern in Salem. John had publicly accused the sick girls of lying. Later, the Proctors' servant Mary Warren provided **evidence** against them. They were found guilty. Elizabeth Proctor was pregnant at her trial. She remained in jail until her release in 1693. John was killed. Minister George Burroughs was also accused. He had been a minister in Salem before the trials began.

George Burroughs was found guilty in 1692.

How Fear Shaped the Trials

TRUTH OR MYTH?

1. **SALEM WAS NOT THE FIRST CITY IN THE COLONIES TO HAVE A WITCH PANIC.**

In 1626, Joan Wright was the first English colonist accused of witchcraft. She lived in the colony of Virginia. Many others were accused before the Salem panic. Salem residents would have heard about these cases.

2. **RELIGIOUS FEAR ALONE CAUSED THE SALEM WITCH PANIC.**

Most people in Salem were Puritans. They followed a religion called Puritanism. This religion had a lot of rules. Everyone had to follow them. If something bad happened, they blamed the devil. They also blamed witchcraft on the devil. Puritans didn't trust anyone who wasn't a Puritan. This led to people accusing non-Puritans of witchcraft.

PEOPLE ACCUSED FAMILY MEMBERS OF WITCHCRAFT TO STAY ALIVE.

Accused witches who blamed others were usually kept alive. Margaret Jacobs confessed. She then said her grandfather, George Jacobs Sr., was also a witch. He was found guilty and killed in August 1692. Margaret later admitted she lied.

Puritans in the colonies of North America leave church in the 1600s.

THE MYTH

RELIGIOUS FEAR ALONE CAUSED THE SALEM WITCH PANIC.

Religious fear played a big role in the panic. Almost everyone believed witches were real. But it wasn't the only cause of the panic. Life in the colonies was difficult. The winter of 1692 was one of the coldest in years. People got sick. Some died. Colonists in Maine fought wars with **Indigenous** people. Salem villagers feared the devil would bring war to their town. Villagers who lived on the outskirts of society were also distrusted. These fears made people more likely to believe witchcraft was at play. Fear spread like a sickness.

Land troubles also made villagers uneasy. The Putnam family fought over land with the Towne family. Ann Putnam Jr. said 71-year-old Rebecca Nurse bewitched her. Nurse was born a Towne. Putnam probably overheard her family talk about this conflict. She may have accused Nurse because of her family's land troubles.

Sailor John Alden Jr. (right) was accused of witchcraft in May 1692.

Salem itself had two parts. Farmers controlled the rural Village. Merchants lived in the seaport, called Salem Town. The Putnams wanted the Village to become its own town. The Porter family had businesses in the Village and in Salem Town. They wanted Salem to remain united. Members of these households accused each other of witchcraft.

The Court

1. A SPECIAL COURT WAS MADE JUST FOR THE SALEM TRIALS.

Massachusetts' governor William Phips established the court on May 27, 1692. The court was called Oyer and Terminer. *Oyer and terminer* means "to hear and determine." Lieutenant Governor William Stoughton ran the court. Eight other men in the colony served as judges.

2. ALL PEOPLE ARRESTED FOR WITCHCRAFT GOT A TRIAL.

The court held hundreds of trials. Some lasted only a few minutes. The first trials took place in the Village's meetinghouse. Later, the trials moved to the courthouse in Salem Town.

3. JURY MEMBERS WERE ASKED TO RECONSIDER TRIAL TESTIMONY.

A **jury** found Rebecca Nurse innocent of witchcraft. Stoughton asked the jury to reconsider part of Nurse's **testimony**. The jury changed their decision to guilty. Nurse was killed on July 19, 1692.

FACT

Judge Nathaniel Saltonstall quit after the first trial. He thought it was unfair.

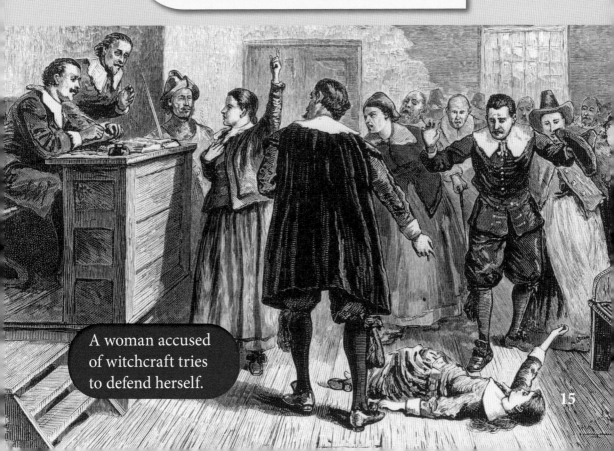

A woman accused of witchcraft tries to defend herself.

THE MYTH

ALL PEOPLE ARRESTED FOR WITCHCRAFT GOT A TRIAL.

Most accused witches did not get trials. The court moved very slowly. Many waited in jails for weeks or months. Some broke out and fled. Others died waiting. Sarah Osborn died in the Boston jail on May 10, 1692.

Farmer Giles Corey and his wife, Martha, sat in jail for months. The jury **convicted** Martha. Giles entered a plea of not guilty. He then refused to participate in his trial.

Because he refused to speak at his trial, officials tortured Giles. They made him lie on the ground. They placed heavy stones on his body. The stones crushed him to death. Martha was put to death on September 22, 1692.

Martha Corey suffered in jail for many months after her conviction.

FACT

Some accused witches waiting for trials were held at the Salem Jail. It was dirty and infested with rats.

Evidence and Punishments

1. WITCH'S MARKS COULD BE USED AS PROOF OF WITCHCRAFT.

Puritans believed the devil left marks on witches. They thought any raised bump, like a mole, might be a witch's mark. Authorities said they found a witch's mark on the finger of 4-year-old Dorothy Good. It could have been a flea bite.

2. SPECTRAL EVIDENCE, SUCH AS VISIONS OR DREAMS, HELPED CONVICT ACCUSED WITCHES.

The sick girls said unseen spirits of witches hurt them. They said the accused flew over their beds at night. Their spirits even attacked them at court. Only the girls could see or feel them. The accused had no way to prove their innocence.

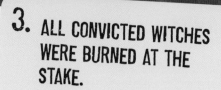

3. ALL CONVICTED WITCHES WERE BURNED AT THE STAKE.

Officials burned convicted witches to make sure no magic remained. They didn't want the magic to spread. The burnings took place in the town's center. Anyone could watch.

THE MYTH

ALL CONVICTED WITCHES WERE BURNED AT THE STAKE.

In Europe, it was common for people convicted of witchcraft to be burned at the stake. But not in Salem.

In Salem, convicted witches were hanged. First, they were driven in carts to the **gallows**. Ministers asked them to confess. None did. George Burroughs even said the Lord's Prayer perfectly. It was said that a witch would not be able to say this prayer. He was hanged anyway.

For many years, it was believed the hangings took place at Gallows Hill. Historians later placed the hangings at a hill called Proctor's Ledge.

FACT

The city of Salem bought the land at Proctor's Ledge. In 2016, a memorial was built there.

After saying the Lord's Prayer, George Burroughs was hanged on August 19, 1692.

How Food Played a Role

1. THE SALEM WITCH PANIC BEGAN WHEN YOUNG GIRLS GOT ERGOT POISONING.

Ergot poisoning is a type of food poisoning. The young girls ate poisoned rye bread. This caused them to see things that weren't really there. Once they stopped eating the bread, their visions stopped.

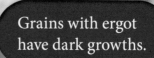

Grains with ergot have dark growths.

2. TITUBA BAKED A WITCH'S CAKE MADE WITH THE SICK GIRLS' URINE.

In early 1692, Tituba baked a witch's cake with the sick girls' urine. She fed it to a dog to reveal any witchcraft at play. Soon, Betty and Abigail accused Tituba of witchcraft. She confessed. Historians believe Samuel Parris forced Tituba to confess.

3. ACCUSED WITCHES HAD TO PAY FOR THEIR OWN FOOD IN JAIL.

The accused waited in jail until trial. They were locked in metal chains. They had to pay for their own food, clothing, blankets, and firewood. If they couldn't afford food, they didn't eat.

THE MYTH

THE SALEM WITCH PANIC BEGAN WHEN YOUNG GIRLS GOT ERGOT POISONING.

Ergot poisoning can cause visions, dizziness, and shaking. But the idea that the Salem girls had ergot poisoning has been disproven. The accusers ate the same bread as their families. Their family members didn't get sick. Other accusers came from towns outside of Salem. They didn't eat the same bread as the Salem girls.

The Salem girls were sometimes symptom-free. After Bridget Bishop died, no new suspects were named for two weeks. Ergot poisoning doesn't go away and come back. Historians believe Bishop's death scared the girls.

No one knows why the girls in Salem accused people of witchcraft. They may have truly believed they saw witches. Adults may have pressured them to name more witches. Perhaps they were too afraid to admit they lied. But whatever the reasons, it wasn't bad bread.

After the Trials

1. THE GOVERNOR'S WIFE WAS ACCUSED OF WITCHCRAFT.

Governor Phips's wife was accused in the fall of 1692. Phips quickly shut down the court. In January 1693, the trials started again in regular court. Spectral evidence was banned. Most cases were tossed out. Only three more people were convicted. None died.

2. SOME PEOPLE APOLOGIZED FOR THEIR ROLES IN THE TRIALS.

Judge Samuel Sewall believed those convicted were innocent. He said the devil had tricked him. Several members of the jury also apologized. Accuser Ann Putnam Jr. apologized in 1706.

3. AFTER THE SALEM TRIALS, CHARGES OF WITCHCRAFT ENDED IN THE COLONIES.

The Salem witch trials sent a powerful message to the colonies. Witchcraft was too hard to prove. Killing the innocent was far too easy. Everyone learned their lesson from what happened in Salem.

Samuel Sewall

THE MYTH

AFTER THE SALEM TRIALS, CHARGES OF WITCHCRAFT ENDED IN THE COLONIES.

By May 1693, the Salem witch trials had ended for good. Close to 200 people had been accused of witchcraft. Twenty people were killed. But the fear of witchcraft continued. In 1706, Grace Sherwood of Virginia stood trial for witchcraft. To test Sherwood, the court ordered her to be bound and then tossed into a river. If she sank, she was innocent. Sherwood untied herself and floated to the surface. She spent many years in jail.

FACT

Over time, all convictions in the Salem witch trials were overturned. The last conviction to be cleared was Elizabeth Johnson's in 2022.

More than 300 years ago, fear gripped Salem, Massachusetts. Neighbors accused neighbors of witchcraft. Family and friends turned against one another. The difference between truth and myth grew cloudy. How many myths did you spot on your journey through Salem's witch hunt?

Visitors walk through the Salem Witch Trials Memorial.

GLOSSARY

accuse (uh-KYOOZ)—to say someone has done something wrong; someone who accuses is an accuser

colony (KAH-luh-nee)—a territory settled by people from another country and controlled by that country

confess (kuhn-FESS)—to admit you have done something wrong

convict (KUHN-vikt)—to find someone guilty of a crime

enslave (en-SLAYV)—to force someone to do work without pay

ergot (UR-gut)—a fungus that grows on grains

evidence (EH-vuh-duhnss)—information, items, and facts that help prove something to be true or false

gallows (GAL-ohz)—a wooden frame that holds a rope used to hang criminals

Indigenous (in-DI-juh-nuhs)—a way to describe the first people who lived in a certain area

jury (JUR-ee)—a group of people at a trial that decides if someone is guilty of a crime

testimony (TESS-tuh-moh-nee)—a statement given by a witness who is under oath in a court of law

trial (TRYE-uhl)—the court process to decide if a charge or claim is true

READ MORE

Burgan, Michael. *The Salem Witch Trials: Mass Hysteria and Many Lives Lost*. North Mankato, MN: Capstone, 2019.

Cooke, Tim. *Accused of Witchcraft! Salem, 1692-1693*. Minneapolis: Bearport Publishing Company, 2023.

Silva, Sadie. *The Thirteen Colonies*. Buffalo, NY: Enslow Publishing, 2023.

INTERNET SITES

Ducksters: Colonial America: Salem Witch Trials
ducksters.com/history/colonial_america/salem_witch_trials.php

National Geographic Kids: The Salem Witch Trials
kids.nationalgeographic.com/history/article/salem-witch-trials

Salem Witch Trials of 1692
salem.org/salem-witch-trials

INDEX

Bishop, Bridget, 8, 24
burning at the stake, 19, 20
Burroughs, George, 9, 20, 21

Corey, Giles, 16
Corey, Martha, 16

dogs, 7, 23

ergot poisoning, 22, 24

Good, Dorothy, 7, 18
Good, Sarah, 7, 8

hangings, 20, 21

Jacobs, Margaret, 11

Nurse, Rebecca, 12, 15

Osborn, Sarah, 8, 16

Parris, Samuel, 4, 8, 23
Proctor's Ledge, 20
Puritanism, 10, 11, 18
Putnam, Ann, Jr., 12, 26

Salem Town, 13, 14
Samuel Sewall, 26
Sherwood, Grace, 28
spectral evidence, 18, 26

Tituba, 8, 23

Village, 13, 14

ABOUT THE AUTHOR

Megan Cooley Peterson is a writer, editor, and bookworm. When she isn't writing or reading, you can find her watching movies or planning her next Halloween party. She lives in Minnesota with her husband and daughter.